FAITH

A SURVIVAL GUIDE

FAITH

A SURVIVAL GUIDE

Stewart Keiller

TERRA NOVA PUBLICATIONS

Copyright ©2007 Stewart Keiller

The right of Stewart Keiller to be identified as author of this work has been asserted by him in accordance with the Copyright, Designs and Patents Act 1988.
All rights reserved.
No part of this publication may be reproduced or transmitted in any form or by any means, electronic or mechanical, including photocopy, recording or any information storage and retrieval system, without prior permission in writing from the publisher.

Published in Great Britain by
Terra Nova Publications International Ltd.
Orders and enquiries: PO Box 2400 Bradford on Avon BA15 2YN
Registered Office (not for trade):
21 St.Thomas Street, Bristol BS1 6JS

Scripture quotations marked NIV taken from the
HOLY BIBLE, NEW INTERNATIONAL VERSION,
Copyright © 1973, 1978, 1984 by International Bible Society.
Used by permission of Hodder & Stoughton,
a member of the Hodder Headline Group.
All rights reserved.

Scripture quotations marked (NKJV) are taken from the
New King James Version
Copyright © 1982, by Thomas Nelson, Inc.
Used by permission. All rights reserved.

Scripture quotations marked (AMP) are taken from the Amplified Bible, Old Testament. Copyright © 1965, 1987, by the Zondervan Corporation. The Amplified New Testament, copyright © 1954, 1958, 1987 by The Lockman Foundation. Used by permission.

Scripture quotations marked NLT are taken from the
Holy Bible, New Living Translation, copyright 1996, 2004.
Used by permission of Tyndale House Publishers, Inc., Wheaton, Illinois 60189. All rights reserved.

ISBN 978 1 901949 49 0

Printed in Great Britain
by Bookmarque Ltd, Croydon

Dedication

In the service of the King
extending his kingdom

Contents

How can *I* have faith?	9
Substance and evidence	11
Making faith work	15
God speaks	19
Faith principle	23
A story about Abel	25
Enoch — a disappearing act	29
Noah the boat builder	33
Father Abraham	37
When God takes his time	41
Passing the baton	47
So what is the survival guide?	53
Bible guide	57

How can I have faith?

There is a television programme where a group of people are sent off into the jungle and a camera follows them to see how they are doing. I have thought it would be cool to do one of those jungle expeditions with our church: send ten of us off to the jungle, and each week we could have a little clip of how we are doing! We would find a survival guide really helpful. In what follows, I am going to give you one key point which I believe will be your survival guide for the jungle that is this world we live in, but you have to take it in and then act on it.

Have a look at this verse in Hebrews. This is a declaration: '. . . but we are not of those who shrink back and are destroyed, but of those who believe and are saved. Now faith is being sure of what we hope for and certain of what we do not see. This is what the ancients were commended for' (Hebrews 10:38–11:1, NIV). I love that. We are not those who are going to shrink back to the jungle of life, but we are going to be those who are survivors. God has not called us to shrink back, retreat, hide, run away, curl up and die; no, we are those who are going to believe and be saved —in other words, survive and come alive!

Substance and evidence

Another version of the Bible translates it, '. . . faith is the substance of things hoped for, the evidence of things not seen' (NKJV). *Substance* and *evidence* are two key words here. Substance really means something that lies underneath and gives support. You are probably sitting in a chair as you read this, just try bouncing up and down .... Now I know you may be reading this on a bus or in a coffee shop, but nevertheless have a bounce. Test what you are sitting on – GO ON! Feel what that support is like. It is something that lies underneath you. Faith is like that, it supports something on top. Evidence is something that needs to be proven and tested; evidence is necessary to establish something is true.

We don't necessarily see evidence with our senses. The Amplified Version really opens up our understanding of this, in the expression 'faith perceiving as real fact what is not revealed to the senses'. In our lives we deal with the senses all the time. We live in a very sensual world, stimulating our senses by what we see and hear. However, I have begun to learn that not everything which is real can be perceived by physical senses. When the Holy Spirit comes and lives inside us, we get the Spirit's sense working in us; in fact, there is a whole realm of the spirit to which we are now alert and alive.

SUBSTANCE AND EVIDENCE

> **Question**
> How do we access 'life in the Spirit' and come to understand the dynamics of living in this unseen realm?
>
> **Answer**
> By maturing and sharpening our spiritual senses, not our physical senses.

So we see in Hebrews 11:1 that faith is something of substance, something of certainty, and something that gives us evidence. Now for many years I've had the view that I have got to work faith up on the inside of me, I've got to believe hard enough somehow for it to work. And, if I can believe enough, I might just get access to this supernatural mountain-moving realm. I sort of thought that faith was a bit like this: if I could get it exactly the right strength, with the right words, it would work! Have you thought a bit like this — or is it just me? JUST BELIEVE BADLY ENOUGH! IF I JUST BELIEVE ENOUGH, IT'S ALL GOING TO WORK OUT! But, funnily enough, you don't actually believe. No matter how hard you try to work yourself up to think this, you just can't make faith. Working hard at believing doesn't seem to work.

Making faith work

So how does this faith idea work? It is supposed to be substance to our lives, something that we can rely on, something that's firm like the floor underneath us — this invisible faith thing which we've got to depend on; and what's more the Bible says that there is evidence to back it up. It is not something which we evidence by touching and feeling, because the kingdom of God, of course, is within us. The Bible says that the kingdom is 'at hand', but it also says it is within you. How can we get this faith thing, this invisible thing, into something which really is substance and evidence for our lives?

Look at Hebrews 11:3. 'By faith we understand that the universe was formed at God's command, so that what is seen was not made out of what was visible' (NIV). [The word there for 'command' is *rhema*.] What does that mean? Everything that you are looking at now, everything that is visible to your eyes, was birthed from something that could not be seen, something invisible. Remember that Hebrews and Genesis sort of go along with each other. In Genesis, God is at work, he uses his words to create stuff, he says 'let there be light', and light came about! Cool. Something from the invisible realm, the spiritual realm, suddenly became visible. At what? The command of God, the rhema word of God. Rhema word? There are two Greek words in Scripture translated into the English 'word': *logos* and *rhema*. Rhema is that 'now' word that God is speaking, his utterance: the now current — vital, full of life — word.

The rhema word came: God spoke and

creation was formed. Romans 10:17 says that, '... faith comes by hearing, and hearing by the word of God' (NKJV). That is a key verse of Scripture! If you want faith to be substance and evidence, you have to get faith from the word. We have to get faith from a rhema word, a word that Father God is speaking now, from what God is saying to you – yes, *you*! And look, it is not about working yourself up enough to believe. What is it about? Hearing what God is saying to us, today! When I found that out, suddenly the lights came on for me. I know now that I don't have to work myself up and be a really good godly believer and live this life of faith *first*. No, what I have to do first is listen, and hear what God is saying today.

God speaks

So how does God speak to us? Well, one way God speaks to us is through prophecies. At our church you can book yourself in for a time of prophetic encouragement. As I write this, I think of a fantastic time I had at such a meeting recently. They had a spare place and I went. Poor guys! I said, 'Prophesy over me', and they did. It was great — spot on. I heard the *now* word of God. The word of God comes from that prompting on the inside; the word of God comes from one another; and sometimes the word of God comes through our circumstances. (Not always, just sometimes.) But the most important way is that the word of God comes from the Bible.

Now I love the funny and powerful ways the Holy Spirit works among us, but the word doesn't only come through the manifestation of the Spirit's work as we move in his gifts. Certainly, when the Holy Spirit comes, he really speaks to us. But you cannot expect the Holy Spirit to build a substance and foundation in your life unless you are growing in the word of God, the Bible.

Without the Spirit, the Bible can seem, well frankly boring — as dull as dishwater! In fact, if you study the Bible without the Holy Spirit it just loses the life. But with the Holy Spirit it all comes to life. That rhema word just hits you! How is it that you can read this book over and over and over again, without it getting dull? Because of the Holy Spirit! Life comes through the word.

God loves us to have experience. If we have to live this Christian life without personal experience of the Holy Spirit, it is very hard. I've tried it and I didn't like it! So experience is good, perhaps you can go so far as to say essential to our Christian life. But we need word *and* Spirit. We need both the word of God in Scripture and the Holy Spirit at work in our hearts and amongst us.

Because the Bible is Holy Spirit inspired and 'breathed', it is vibrant, real and authentic. If you don't read the Bible frequently, I really encourage you to open it and read it. If you have a translation you don't understand, throw it away and get one you do understand. Christian bookshops have an array of translations, get one that grips you and is on your level. Some of them may be more accurate translations than others, and some use more contemporary language than others, but the main thing is to read it, and let it work on the inside of you. You don't have to read big chunks of it, start with a few passages. I can guarantee that when you do that, with the Holy Spirit, something will spring to life in the words.

Faith principle

So here is the principle, and then I am going to apply this principle to the rest of Hebrews. The principle is this:

God speaks

We receive

Faith is generated

We act on it

That is the *survival guide*. If you get that inside you and start to act on it, then something will happen — that is guaranteed.

A story about Abel

Look now at what is said about Abel. 'By faith Abel offered God a better sacrifice than Cain did. By faith he was commended as a righteous man, when God spoke well of his offerings...' (Hebrews 11:4a, NIV).

Remember the Survival Guide: God speaks; we receive; faith is generated; act on it — and suddenly up comes Abel. Why on earth Abel? Abel is a bit obscure, to say the least. What did Abel do? Abel and Cain — what brotherly love! We assume they heard God somehow, God communicated with Adam (dad), Eve (mum), Cain and Abel, and there was something going on in the garden (you can read it all in Genesis 4:2–5). God clearly spoke to Abel because he knew he needed to make an offering. This passage in Hebrews shows us that the sacrifice and offerings were significant. God spoke somehow, and Abel got the message about making an offering. Now what is offering? Offering is giving the best. The thing that distinguished Cain from Abel was that Abel gave his best — he gave God his first-born lamb; he brought to God the best. He understood what it was to give God everything — to give him the best. God spoke, Abel received it, and something happened on the inside of him. How do we know? Because it talks about Abel acting in faith. What did it say? 'By faith Abel offered a better sacrifice than Cain did' (NIV). By *faith*.

Have you ever thought about righteous actions? When God looks at us, he doesn't look at our righteous actions, he looks at the root of faith that stimulates action. God is interested in the faith. In fact, a little later on, in Hebrews 11:6, it says, 'And without faith it is impossible to please God, because anyone who comes to him must believe that he exists and that he rewards those who earnestly seek him' (NIV). So if you are just *trying your hardest* to please God at this precise moment, then I suggest you take to heart that it is impossible to please God just by *effort* — because what you need is faith. Actions should always come out of faith. God speaks, we receive, and faith is generated. That's it! We have to do something with the faith that is generated. The faith produced in us will change our attitudes and behaviour. Here you see Abel's attitude change because he brought a wonderful sacrificial offering. He brought his best to God. Something came alive on the inside of him, and he just brought the very, very best.

But here the rubber hits the road: responding to God can cost you everything. In fact for Abel it cost him his life! Now I am not suggesting for a minute that stepping out on God's word will cost us our actual lives

– though there are places in the world where this happens. But it is worth stopping for a minute and contemplating the cost that you are prepared to take for the sake of God's word to you. As you are prepared to go out on a limb and give your very best for God, there is a devil out there who will go out on a limb to oppose your faith-motivated action. Don't be 'sweet talked' into some idea that everything will be great fun and you will be safe — Jesus required his disciples to drop everything and follow him. It is a journey of adventure and a life of challenge resulting in the uncovering of your destiny and fulfilment — but it will never be safe! Still want to take faith-motivated action?

Enoch
— a disappearing act

If you thought that Abel was an obscure character to help illustrate the meaning of faith, how about the next one! 'It was by faith that Enoch was taken up to heaven without dying' (Hebrews 11:5, NLT). He disappeared because God took him. Before he was taken up, he was known as a person who 'pleased' God. Now, there are only around four verses about Enoch in the whole Bible. (You will find them in Genesis 5:21–24.) Enoch was 'buddies' with God. One day he was walking along with his Heavenly Father, the two of them were chatting intensely about the state of the world or something, the way good friends do, and he disappeared from sight. When you have fellowship with God and are close to God, you can chat away to him and find yourself in a different place, lifted from the problems. This is an amazing story, because suddenly there is a move from the physical realm to the spiritual realm, in the blink of an eye! I think we see Jesus doing something similar: one minute he is praying to the Father and suddenly he finds himself walking on the water — that sounds great fun!

We can get to a place with the Father where the physical stuff starts to change because of our relationship with him. Think about healing. You know we don't have to 'conjure up' healing — 'Now I'm going to PRAY for somebody.' It should be the overflow of what is in the inside of us. (Remember, the kingdom of God is within.) It should be the overflow of that spiritual life on the inside which punctures the physical on the outside.

So that's Enoch. Remember: the only

way to please God is by faith. And Enoch's righteousness was only righteous because of the faith that he lived in.

Noah the boat builder

Let us move on to Noah in Hebrews 11:7. It says of Noah that he 'walked in close fellowship with God'. (See Genesis 6:9, NLT.) In fact, it goes a bit further in the scripture and it says that Noah was the only righteous man in the world at the time! Noah was not righteous because of what he did — it was the faith in him. He heard God's word; he received it; faith did its stuff on the inside of him, and then he acted upon it. God spoke to Noah, and Noah learnt that God was going to wipe out rebellious, sinful mankind. So God gave him plans to build a boat. In fact he built the biggest man-made structure that was ever known on the face of the planet at that time. He did something completely out of the box. God spoke (rhema word); faith was created; and Noah acted on that faith, despite what must have been the ridicule and the criticism. Can you imagine building an ark in your back garden? And everyone says: 'What are you doing? Are you making a shed for your tools? What is it?' Noah stepped out on the word that God had given him. Now don't think that it was somehow different for Noah in those days. He had no more access to God than we do today, in fact we have more! But he walked with God, and faith was generated on the inside of him. He didn't have to work himself up into a fervour to build that ark. He built it because God spoke to him, the word was inside him. And in verse 7 it says that Noah condemned mankind by his faithful actions. Fancy having that on your epitaph! 'Stewart Keiller condemned mankind because of his faithful actions!' He chose to believe in God rather than the circumstances around him; he chose to respond to the word of God that came and dwelt inside him —he received it; faith was generated, and he operated on that basis, not on the basis of what everyone else around him said.

If you get hold of this principle – that we need to hear what God says and receive it, ruminate on it, let it permeate, percolate and pickle us – then, when you start stepping out on it, you might look strange to others! But you know what happens: God is going to come alongside you, give you strength, provide the answer, sustain you —because he loves it when we act on faith.

Father Abraham

Then we have Abraham in Hebrews 11:8–12, paralleled in Genesis 12. He was told by God to, '. . . go to the land I will show you' (Genesis 12:1b). Now, you have to go back in the story a bit. Abraham's father, Terah, had set out for Canaan. We don't know that God spoke to him, but there is an implication here that possibly God had spoken to that man to start the process. (See the end of Genesis 11.)

Let us use our imagination and think of a situation we can all identify with! Think of Terah driving down the motorway (freeway to any Americans reading) to Canaan, needing some petrol (gas). He was a bit thirsty, too, so he stopped at the service station along the way. He stopped at this place called Haran — 'Haran Services'. So here we are, Abraham's dad Terah stops, the family get out of their camper van, and they have cappuccinos and a takeaway. The problem is that they stayed there too long. In fact they decided that the service station was so nice that they set up permanent camp in the car park! So there is a point where God's word comes again. This time God didn't bother with the dad. In Genesis 12 the word comes to Abraham: 'Go to a country I am going to show you.' So he gets up and goes. As a little aside, I wonder how many of us are enjoying takeaways and cappuccinos in what is a service station. Are we living in the land that we have been promised? Have you taken the land that you are supposed to take? Or have we just settled for a cappuccino and a takeaway? Have some of us, maybe 'fathers in the faith', settled for 'fast food' when we set out for a banquet? Well, I'm not settling for a takeaway. Don't settle; don't get into a lay-by; don't get sidelined —because if you do that you will miss the bigger thing. And what's the bigger thing? Look at Hebrews 11:10 — a heavenly home. When God spoke, he put something inside Abraham which was a heavenly home, a bigger place, a place that he would be going to. God put inside Abraham such a vision for something that he was desperate to get there. Abraham just desired the better place — the car park was not what was in his heart. God gave him a picture of something that was ahead, and that was the thing he lived for. Let God put a big picture inside you! Let him paint a big picture about where you are going. Let him put something amazing inside you, and then aim for it.

Now the story doesn't stop there, because poor old Sarah and Abraham didn't have any kids. Now that is pretty sad for a couple in our culture. For people who really want children it is desperate —but in that culture it was terrible, in fact it was like a curse. And yet God promised them kids, so much so that Abraham argues with him about it. In Genesis 15:21 he keeps arguing, but God keeps speaking the word about having descendants, and Abraham goes on having this debate with him. But Abraham actually received the word about having children. And there's a lovely verse, Genesis 15:6, where it says, 'Abram believed the Lord, and he credited it to him as righteousness' (NIV), because Abraham heard the word, and in his conversations with God he let it settle in his spirit, and faith emerged. He stepped out on the basis of believing that God was going to give him a son.

When God takes his time

Later on, Abraham even tried to help God along the way a bit. You know how it is when it seems that God takes his time? Have you had that experience of God taking ages to do something he had promised, sometimes it doesn't quite happen at the pace you had hoped it would happen? Well, Abraham and Sarah had that experience. They were getting on a bit and probably thinking, 'Oh, we haven't had our kid yet.' How many of us, at the age of ninety-eight, would be thinking that? It was suggested that perhaps what was needed was for Abraham to sleep with the maid, and then they would basically adopt the child and that would fulfil what God had said.

So they planned it all out as best as they could and Ishmael was born. I have certainly felt like giving God a hand on more than a few occasions, and this had seemed to be a good plan. When God brings his word, we receive it and faith is generated, and sometimes by our actions we try to make it happen — watch it, or you will end up with an 'Ishmael'. However, God is loving and forgiving, and despite the fact that Abraham and Sarah had this Ishmael problem, God's heart was still for them. Soon enough, they got their own child — the right way. In the midst of ridicule, because frankly they were past it, here was the family of God taking shape.

In the midst of when it's inconvenient; in the midst of when it makes little sense; in the midst of where it costs you your dignity; in the midst of the darkest place, you can rely – absolutely, firmly rely – on God. This is faith. If you have heard the word of God for your life, you have received it, and faith has been generated, you can be sure to step out on that word.

So that is Abraham. A number of years ago I was in business, and actually doing quite well. In the church, people would have said of me, 'Stewart's quite a good businessman.' I employed staff, including quite a few church members. (It can be very hard having people in the church working for you, because you've got to be on your best behaviour all the time! I didn't do that very well!) God spoke to me and said that I was going through a three-year training course; and I thought: What! Do you want me to leave my job and go to a university or something?

'No, you are on a three-year training course.'

I said, 'Okay, Lord, I'll do that. I'll treat this business as a three-year training course if that's what you want me to do.' And that word stuck with me. I actually stepped out on it, knowing that there was a timescale on it of three years. So I set about building a very important business and raised a million pounds of capital for a venture. I had a nice big office with a great big table. I felt very important. Did my ego a world of good! Except two years later we had to liquidate the company. In fact, I had three businesses and they all went bust at the same time. So there I am, and lo and behold it's the end of the three-year period, with God's words ringing in my ears. I'm thinking: 'Well, thank you very much God, that was a very expensive training course!' I was cross, to say the least!

God spoke to me again and he said, 'Don't look back on it now, but in six months' time you'll understand.' I thought 'Okay', so I took that word at face value, decided not to feel too sorry for myself, and acted on that word. Six months later I was asked to join the leadership team at the church. Now you can look back on it, and you can say you just sort of fit in the events to fit in with your plan. But, as clear as anything, those words that came to me — I received them. God spoke, I received them, faith was generated in me during that three-year period and in the six-month period, and I chose to step out on those words. My plan had been to help God along a bit — become a millionaire, live off the interest, and then I could do whatever the Lord wanted me to do. Well, God didn't actually like my plan! I thought it was a great plan (I am sure Abraham was pretty happy with the plan they concocted!), but I'd rather do God's plan, because when I try to do my version of his plan it will never quite work out the way I want it to.

Passing the baton

In Hebrews 11 there is much more. Verses 13–16 are just brilliant. Have a look at verse 13, 'All these people were still living by faith when they died' (NIV). [The NLT says, '. . . still believing what God had promised them.'] 'They did not receive the things promised; they only saw them and welcomed them from a distance . . . .' Well, in a way I don't like that verse! I want to receive what I am in faith for! I've got faith, I want to see it, and I want to see it now, Lord, please! But verse 13 is key, because society conditions us to believe that 'it's all about you!' It is not all about us. The 'all about you' advertisement is a lie. It is about God! It's about Jesus coming for his bride. It's about us as the company of God's people coming together. Now verse thirteen is a really important scripture. If you look back at the heroes of faith in this chapter of Hebrews, you can see that they realized in their lives some of what they saw and dreamed for. They saw a taster, a down payment. Now I think when God puts something in our hearts and we step out on it, it doesn't automatically follow that we are going to be the ones to see it. We may not see the fulfilment of what God says in our lives. We should still live our lives in total pursuit of the vision, but if you don't see it all fulfilled you are neither a failure nor have you missed God's calling.

In Scripture we read stories about fathers and sons. (I use this in a spiritual sense rather than in the sense of peculiar to men. Women, this includes you — you are, after all, sons of God, sharers in the inheritance.) In fact, the bulk of Scripture is a history of the generations passing between father and son — people of

God. God is interested in the movement from one generation to another. Fathers and sons are supposed to run the race together. When you pass the baton, you don't run up to the person, stop, give them the baton, they pick it up and then they start running. No, there's always that bit where you are running together, isn't there? And that is how we are supposed to be: fathers running, passing on to the sons. We are supposed to run this race together, passing the baton as we go. There is something transferable about vision. God can speak to you about something, you have a passion for it in God, and you may get something established, but maybe it is your sons – spiritual sons – who should pick it up and run with it.

I want to be part of a church where there are fathers and sons working together; and where we pass the baton to one another, passing on the spiritual inheritance that came through faith, passing on the vision to the next generation. You may only see it from afar and welcome the vision, but the Spirit is at work in us, and he is the master planner. Let us get his perspective, live with this dimension of the Spirit. Change your perspective to a kingdom one. Ever been up a mountain and you see things differently? If we go up high, our perspectives on the physical world change. Any vision we have been given by Father is actually a jigsaw piece fulfilled in this wonderful, connected body that comes together — the church. You know, we don't just live our lives for our generation, but for every generation to come, as well.

Hebrews 11:40, 'For God had something better in mind for us, so that they would not reach perfection without us' (NLT). This chapter, having listed the heroes of the faith, then teaches me that they would not become perfect without me. We are part of an inheritance that comes from the earliest parts of Scripture, an inheritance of faith that comes from one generation to the next. The story is not going to be complete without you and your contribution. Try to get a handle on this idea: each one of us has to play our part. We need to go to God and get the word for our lives; receive that word of God, really hear it; let it brew away on the inside, and then act upon it. When we do that, we are stepping into an inheritance of faith; over the generations and generations this wonderful body starts to come together. You are important in global history – that's what that verse is actually showing – for they (the past heroes of faith) would not reach perfection without you.

So what is the survival guide?

You can take what I have said and apply it to whatever you are facing at the moment — whatever circumstances, whatever difficulties, whatever crises confront you. You don't have to work faith up and somehow make it happen.

Here's how we do it, the survival guide of faith —when the rubber hits the road in the morning; when you wake up in a bad mood; when your circumstances say, 'we haven't got anything to pay the bills'; when somebody is sick around you; when you're sick; when life looks particularly miserable. In the midst of it all, the survival guide is this: God speaks;

we receive; faith does its stuff on the inside of us. Let faith do its stuff. And what do we do? Act on what he has said. That's it!

People of faith, let's not be ones who shrink back and are destroyed, but let's be the ones who press forward. You know, it isn't about working up a sweat to become 'faith people', it's about responding to the very word of God, letting it do something on the inside of us and acting on what he has said.

BIBLE GUIDE

BIBLE PASSAGES TO THINK ABOUT

. . . but we are not of those who shrink back and are destroyed, but of those who believe and are saved. Now faith is being sure of what we hope for and certain of what we do not see. This is what the ancients were commended for (Hebrews 10:38–11:1, NIV).

. . . faith is the substance of things hoped for, the evidence of things not seen (Hebrews 11:1, NKJV).

By faith we understand that the universe was formed at God's command, so that what is seen was not made out of what was visible (Hebrews 11:3, NIV).

. . . faith comes by hearing, and hearing by the word of God (Romans 10:17, NKJV).

By faith Abel offered God a better sacrifice than Cain did. By faith he was commended as a righteous man . . . (Hebrews 11:4a, NIV).

And without faith it is impossible to please God, because anyone who comes to him must believe that he exists and that he rewards those who earnestly seek him (Hebrews 11:6, NIV).

It was by faith that Enoch was taken up to heaven without dying (Hebrews 11:5, NLT).

[Noah] walked in close fellowship with God. (See Genesis 6:9, NLT.)

All these people were still living by faith when they died (Hebrews 11:13, NIV).

For God had something better in mind for us, so that they would not reach perfection without us (Hebrews 11:40, NLT).

BY THE SAME AUTHOR

PURSUING A HEAVENLY VISION

ISBN 978 1 901949 57 5

192pp UK £7.99

- Do you feel God has put a burden in you?
- Do you sense destiny on your life?
- Do you want to know that what you do on earth has eternal significance?
    —then this book is for you.

'What makes me excited about Pursuing a Heavenly Vision *is that Stewart's message is relating vision and destiny within the context of the Father's love and the Spirit of God's voice.'*

Marc Dupont

In *Pursuing a Heavenly Vision* Stewart Keiller lifts the lid on God's calling and destiny for our lives. We are shown how to get clarity and conviction about what God is calling us to be and do — rather than just following a hunch or idea. This down-to-earth teaching shows how you can access spiritual realms without going all fluffy and ethereal. Stewart's conviction is that God wants to speak to us, in fact *is* speaking to us about our heavenly destiny — it is not all shrouded in mystery but is accessible.

Available from Christian bookshops

www.terranovapress.com

RESOURCES
FROM BATH CITY CHURCH

CDs (prices include UK p & p)

KAIROS
Stewart Keiller £9 CD-006-KAI

Time passing you by? Missed the moment? Redeem the time and appreciate the seasons of the soul.

FAITH WORKS
Stewart Keiller & Stephen Wood £11 CD-012-FAI

How to take everyday decisions from a place of confidence in what God has said to you.

MAKING A DIFFERENCE
Stewart Keiller & Stephen Wood £11 CD-005-DIF

God has a plan for you: he wants you to fulfil the dreams he has given you, using the power of the Holy Spirit to help you live it.

NO GUTS NO GLORY!
Stewart Keiller £11 CD-011-GUT

Challenges men to be the men God created them to be, and to do what God has called them to do.

THE ANCHOR OF HOPE
Stewart Keiller £5 CD-010-HOP

Feeling tossed about by the storms of life? Find out how to lay hold of hope —the anchor we need.

WHOM SHALL I FEAR?
Stewart Keiller £5 CD-009-FEA

Afraid? The threat from terror? Your circumstances? Access the resources of heaven and find a place of peace.

To order online, visit: **www.bathcitychurch.org.uk**

Telephone +44(0)1225 463556
Fax +44(0)1225 460651